STARS OF PRO WRESTLING

UNDERTAKER

BY TIM O'SHEI

Consultant:
Mike Johnson, Writer
PWInsider.com

Capstone
press®

Mankato, Minnesota

Edge Books are published by Capstone Press,
151 Good Counsel Drive, P.O. Box 669, Mankato, Minnesota 56002.
www.capstonepress.com

Books published by Capstone Press are manufactured with paper
containing at least 10 percent post-consumer waste.

Library of Congress Cataloging-in-Publication Data
O'Shei, Tim.
    Undertaker / by Tim O'Shei.
    p. cm. — (Edge books. Stars of pro wrestling)
    Includes bibliographical references and index.
    Summary: "Describes the life and career of pro wrestler the Undertaker"
— Provided by publisher.
    ISBN 978-1-4296-3351-2 (library binding)
    1. Undertaker, 1965– — Juvenile literature. 2. Wrestlers — United States
— Biography — Juvenile literature. I. Title.
GV1196.U54O74 2010
796.812092 — dc22   2008055953

Editorial Credits
Angie Kaelberer, editor; Ted Williams, designer; Jo Miller, media researcher

Photo Credits
Corbis/Duomo, 26
Getty Images Inc./Russell Turiak, 10; WireImage/Kevin Mazur, cover;
    WireImage/Leon Halip, 7
Globe Photos, 18; Allstar/Graham Whitby-Boot, 13; John Barrett, 9, 16,
    20, 27, 29; Milan Ryba, 17, 22
Newscom, 5; Icon SMI/CITYFILES/Alexandre Pona, 23; MCT/Orlando
    Sentinel/Jacob Langston, 15; Splash News and Pictures/Heather
    Rousseau, 25

Design Elements
Shutterstock/amlet; Henning Janos; J. Danny; kzww

The author thanks Michelle McNamara for her research assistance.

TABLE OF CONTENTS

Chapter 1

ON A WINNING STREAK

It was April 1, 2007, at Ford Field in Detroit, Michigan. Pro wrestling fans filled the stadium for World Wrestling Entertainment's (WWE) biggest event of the year, WrestleMania.

That night, Undertaker had something he wanted to keep and something he wanted to take. Undertaker wanted to keep his record streak of WrestleMania wins. He wanted to take something that belonged to his opponent, Batista — the World Heavyweight Championship belt.

But Batista wasn't ready to give up the belt. At the bell, he charged, knocking Undertaker into the turnbuckle. Batista slammed Undertaker knee-first into the corner. He threw Undertaker into the ropes, *clotheslined* him, and knocked him out of the ring.

Undertaker wanted to keep his winning streak alive at WrestleMania.

WRESTLING MOVE

clothesline — a wrestler runs toward the opponent with his arm outstretched and smashes his arm into the opponent's neck

Slam! Batista crunched Undertaker's head into the boards. Crash! He threw Undertaker into the steel stairs.

Two minutes into the match, Batista was in full control. He threw Undertaker back into the ring. Twice, Batista tried to pin Undertaker. Twice, Undertaker kicked out.

It took only one boot to change the match. Undertaker raised his foot and kicked Batista to the mat. Undertaker tried for a pin, but Batista kicked out. Then Undertaker leaped onto the top rope. He balanced on the rope before dropping down on Batista, knocking him to the mat. As Batista lay half out of the ring, Undertaker jumped on him, dragging him to the floor below. Batista was stunned, but he managed to bodyslam Undertaker into the announcer's table.

Once more, the men returned to the ring. Both were tired and bloody. But there would be no rest until one was the winner.

Batista wanted to end Undertaker's streak.

Chapter 2

TEXAS ROOTS

Usually the little brother in a family doesn't stand out, but Mark Calaway did. Mark was born March 24, 1965, into a family of five boys. Even though Mark was the youngest, he grew to be much bigger than his brothers. Mark grew to be 6 feet, 8 inches (2 meters) tall.

Mark wasn't just a big kid. He was a big-time athlete. At Waltrip High School in Houston, Texas, he played both football and basketball. After graduating from high school in 1983, he attended and played basketball at Angelina College in Lufkin, Texas. In 1985, he went to Texas Wesleyan University in Fort Worth, Texas. Mark played basketball there too, but another sport had caught his attention.

Mark has been a top athlete his entire life.

WRESTLING FACT

Undertaker is famous for walking on the top ropes of the ring and leaping on his opponents. Usually, only small, lightweight wrestlers can perform such high-diving moves.

Mark defeated Jerry "The King" Lawler to win his first championship.

READY FOR WRESTLING

Texas Wesleyan was near the large city of Dallas. This city was the home of a small but popular pro wrestling company called World Class Championship Wrestling (WCCW). Mark met some of the WCCW wrestlers. They were impressed by his height and athletic ability. Mark was a big guy who could run and move fast. That's important in basketball, but it's rare for a wrestler. Most large wrestlers aren't quick enough to wrestle smaller, speedier guys.

Mark had one year left of college when he decided to quit school for a career in sports. For a while, Mark wanted to play pro basketball in Europe. But a friend convinced him to try pro wrestling first.

A MAN OF MANY NAMES

To become a pro wrestler, Mark knew he had to become stronger. He trained hard in the weight room, packing muscle onto his frame. Eventually he bulked up to 328 pounds (149 kilograms).

Mark got his start by wrestling in small companies for little money. He wrestled under several names, including Mean Mark Callous, Master of Pain, and The Punisher. While working in the United States Wrestling Alliance, Mark won his first championship. He defeated Jerry "The King" Lawler for the Unified Heavyweight Championship. In the National Wrestling Alliance, Mark competed twice for the U.S. Championship. He lost both times, but other chances for success would soon come.

Chapter 3

THE DEAD MAN

Mark knew that to be successful, he needed to get a job with a major pro wrestling company. In 1990, World Wrestling Federation (WWF) owner Vince McMahon hired Mark. The WWF is now called WWE. It's the world's largest pro wrestling company.

McMahon and his staff are masters at creating memorable characters for WWE wrestlers. Many people think Mark's Undertaker character is one of their most successful ever.

An undertaker is someone who runs a funeral home. The term isn't used much today, but it was back in the 1800s. Undertaker dressed like he was from those days. He wore a black, wide-brimmed hat and a long coat. Gongs and haunting organ music marked his eerie entrance to the ring. Undertaker always seemed serious and angry.

Undertaker dressed like he was from the Old West.

SIDEKICKS

For a short time, wrestler Brother Love managed Undertaker. But soon Undertaker had a new manager. His wrestling name was Paul Bearer. A pallbearer is someone who helps carry the casket at a funeral.

Paul Bearer carried an **urn**. Bearer said the urn held Undertaker's magical powers. It had another use too. Sometimes Undertaker used it to hit his opponents.

urn — a container that holds the ashes of a cremated body

WRESTLING FACT

According to Undertaker's story, he can't be killed, because he's already dead!

Undertaker at WrestleMania

WrestleMania is like the Super Bowl of wrestling. No event is bigger. And no one has ever dominated WrestleMania quite like Undertaker.

Each of Undertaker's WrestleMania matches has been memorable, but some are considered classics. He wrestled Kane in 1998 and again in 2004. In 2006, Undertaker beat Mark Henry by putting him in a casket. One year later, he beat Batista for the World Heavyweight title. In 2008, Undertaker won the title again with a victory over Edge.

Will Undertaker ever lose at WrestleMania? It doesn't seem likely. But if he does, it will be one of the most shocking stories in wrestling history.

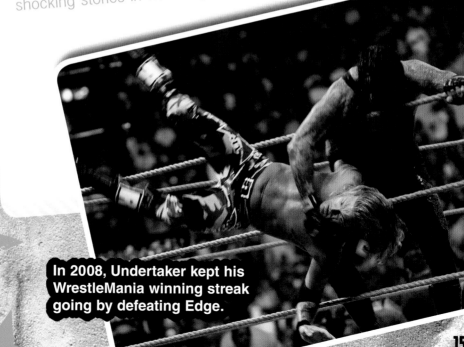

In 2008, Undertaker kept his WrestleMania winning streak going by defeating Edge.

A GREAT BEGINNING

In March 1991, Undertaker wrestled his first WrestleMania match. His opponent was the legendary Jimmy "Superfly" Snuka. Undertaker used his new signature move, the *Tombstone Piledriver*, to defeat Snuka.

Late that same year, Undertaker squared off against another famous wrestler. This man was one of the biggest legends of them all, Hulk Hogan. The World Championship was on the line. The exciting match ended by Undertaker defeating Hogan. It was the first of several title belts Undertaker would win.

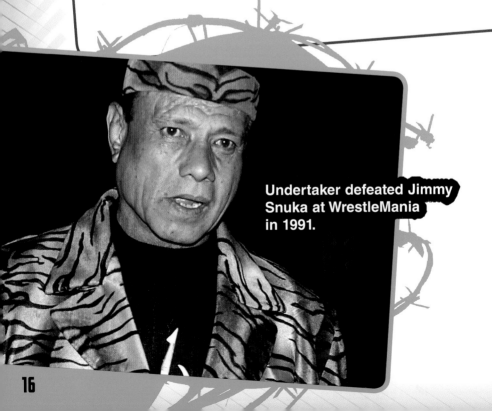

Undertaker defeated Jimmy Snuka at WrestleMania in 1991.

Undertaker slams opponents into submission with the Tombstone Piledriver.

WRESTLING MOVE

Tombstone Piledriver — the wrestler holds the opponent upside down against his stomach and then drops to his knees

Undertaker feuded with Jake "The Snake" Roberts in the early 1990s.

CLASSIC FEUDS

Undertaker is known for his many **feuds**. One of his first was with Jake "The Snake" Roberts. One night, after Roberts defeated Randy "Macho Man" Savage, he turned toward Miss Elizabeth. Miss Elizabeth was Savage's wife and manager. Roberts threatened to hit Elizabeth with a chair, but Undertaker stopped him. That set off a feud with Roberts. It was settled in 1992 at WrestleMania, when Undertaker beat Roberts.

Some of Undertaker's feuds were with Paul Bearer. During a match against Mankind, Undertaker reached toward Bearer. Undertaker wanted his urn. Bearer gave it to him — by hitting Undertaker with it. That set off the first of many splits between Undertaker and Bearer. At one point, Bearer was put into a cage that hung over the ring. Below, Undertaker fought Mankind. If Undertaker won, he would be able to grab Bearer and get his revenge. He did win, but Bearer got lucky. The Executioner stopped Undertaker from getting to his former manager. Despite their many splits, Undertaker and Bearer always reunited until Bearer **retired** from full-time wrestling work in 2005.

feud — a long-running quarrel
retire — to give up a line of work

Kane (right) often wrestled with
and against Undertaker.

DEADLY GIMMICKS

Undertaker had feuds in the 1990s with opponents ranging from Yokozuna to Ted DiBiase. Undertaker often liked to settle matches in creative ways. He locked opponents into caskets or used other **gimmicks** that played off his "deadly" personality. He wrestled in Buried Alive matches, in which the loser was thrown into a fake grave. He also fought in cell matches. In these matches, the two wrestlers were locked in a cage.

In October 1997, Undertaker and Shawn Michaels wrestled in the first cell match. Near the end of the match, a 7-foot (2.1-meter) masked man ripped off the cell door and entered the ring. This wrestler was Kane. He used the Tombstone Piledriver on Undertaker, allowing Michaels to win the match.

Kane's actions began a wrestling relationship with Undertaker that continued for years. At times, they were opponents. Other times, they wrestled as a team. In a famous match, they wrestled in a ring surrounded by leaping flames. Undertaker won the match by setting Kane's arm on fire.

gimmick — a clever trick or idea used to get people's attention

BECOMING A LEGEND

Since joining WWE, Undertaker has wrestled and beaten most of pro wrestling's biggest stars. He defeated legends Jake Roberts, Bret Hart, and Hulk Hogan. He beat current-day stars Triple H, Randy Orton, and Kurt Angle. By defeating all of them, Undertaker became a pro wrestling legend.

In 2005, Undertaker beat Randy Orton at WrestleMania.

Undertaker had some great matches against Triple H (left).

Chapter 4

A WRESTLING LEGEND

On April 1, 2007, Undertaker's undefeated WrestleMania streak and the championship belt were on the line.

In the ring, Undertaker and Batista traded blows. Batista flipped Undertaker onto his shoulders and slammed him to the floor with a *Batista bomb*. But Undertaker kicked out before the referee counted to three.

When Batista tried another Batista bomb, Undertaker twisted out of his grasp. Undertaker slammed Batista into the corner and set him up for the Tombstone Piledriver. As Undertaker smashed Batista's head into the mat, the referee hit the mat and counted to three. Undertaker was once again the World Heavyweight Champion.

Undertaker celebrated winning back the Heavyweight title at WrestleMania in 2007.

WRESTLING MOVE

Batista bomb — the wrestler puts the opponent's head between his thighs, flips the opponent up onto his shoulders, and then drops to the mat with a bodyslam

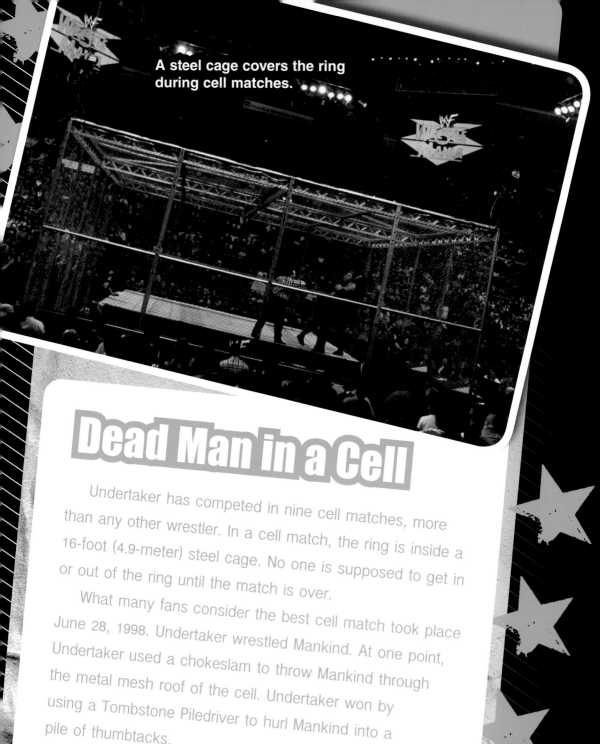

A steel cage covers the ring during cell matches.

Dead Man in a Cell

Undertaker has competed in nine cell matches, more than any other wrestler. In a cell match, the ring is inside a 16-foot (4.9-meter) steel cage. No one is supposed to get in or out of the ring until the match is over.

What many fans consider the best cell match took place June 28, 1998. Undertaker wrestled Mankind. At one point, Undertaker used a chokeslam to throw Mankind through the metal mesh roof of the cell. Undertaker won by using a Tombstone Piledriver to hurl Mankind into a pile of thumbtacks.

HEALTH CHALLENGES

Undertaker has been wrestling since 1986. He has had many injuries. A few times, Undertaker has taken months off to let his injuries heal. He sometimes comes back with a change in his character. Once, Undertaker was off for eight months. When he came back in May 2000, he dropped the "dead man" character. Instead, he wore a leather jacket and bandanna and rode into the ring on a motorcycle. About four years later, he again took time off for health reasons. When he returned, the deadly character was back.

Undertaker's character became a biker in 2000.

MARK IN PRIVATE

When he's not on the road, Mark works on and rides motorcycles. He also enjoys time with his family. He had sons Kevin and Gunner with his first wife, Jodi. He also has two daughters, Chasey and Gracie, with his second wife, Sara.

It's difficult for Mark to get private time. He's so famous that he gets noticed almost everywhere. Once, when touring a school where he might send his kids, he was recognized by a fifth-grader. All of a sudden, kids and staff members crowded around him.

Of course, they're not the only ones who want to be around Undertaker. The wrestling world has focused on Undertaker ever since he made it big in 1990. No matter how much longer he wrestles, he will always be a legend of the sport.

WRESTLING FACT

Undertaker is considered the leader of the WWE locker room. He gives younger wrestlers advice on how to act both in and out of the ring.

Undertaker's long career has
made him a wrestling legend.

GLOSSARY ★ ★ ★ ★ ★ ★

casket (KASS-kit) — a long, narrow box into which a dead person is placed for burial

cremate (KREE-mate) — to burn a dead body to ashes

feud (FYOOD) — a long-running quarrel between two people or groups of people

gimmick (GIM-ik) — a clever trick or idea used to get people's attention

legend (LEJ-uhnd) — someone who is among the best in what they do

phenomenon (fe-NOM-uh-non) — something that is unusual or remarkable

retire (ri-TIRE) — to give up a line of work

revenge (ri-VENJ) — action taken in return for an injury or offense

urn (URN) — a container that holds the ashes of a cremated body

READ MORE

O'Shei, Tim. *Batista.* Stars of Pro Wrestling. Mankato, Minn.: Capstone Press, 2010.

Schaefer, A. R. *The Undertaker: Pro Wrestler Mark Callaway.* Pro Wrestlers. Mankato, Minn.: Capstone Press, 2003.

Shields, Brian, and Kevin Sullivan. *WWE Encyclopedia.* New York: DK, 2009.

INTERNET SITES

FactHound offers a safe, fun way to find Internet sites related to this book. All of the sites on FactHound have been researched by our staff.

Here's all you do:

Visit *www.facthound.com*

FactHound will fetch the best sites for you!

INDEX ★ ★ ★ ★ ★ ★ ★